30 Days

To a Better

Dating Experience

A Mindfulness Program with a Touch of Humor

Logan Tindell

Share your journey!

Let people know you're practicing mindfulness! Post a picture of the cover and include #30DaysNow via social media. Our various guides share the same lessons, so you can see how others are using mindfulness on their journey!

Don't forget that each exercise has a unique hashtag for online sharing.

This book is meant to be a guide only, and does not guarantee specific results. If the lessons and exercises in this book are followed, change can occur for certain people. Results vary from person to person; some people may not need to complete the thirty days to experience change, but it's encouraged that the entire program be read completely through at least once.

The last half of the book consists of blank note pages that the reader can use in conjunction with the exercises for each day. The reader is encouraged to utilize the note pages; though it's not necessary.

Give the gift of mindfulness. See similar guides at www.30DaysNow.com if you wish to purchase a book for a loved one. **See the disclosure below.**

Disclosure (Shared Lessons and Exercises):
Keep in mind that our mindfulness guides share the same lessons and exercises, so there is no need to purchase more than one book; unless you are sharing with a group or giving the guides as gifts. Our mindfulness guides are created for various topics; however, they utilize the same lessons and exercises, so please be aware of this before purchasing. For example, *30 Days to a Better Dating Experience* will mostly have the same lessons and exercises as *30 Days to Reduce Anxiety* and so forth. By reading just one of our guides, you'll be able to apply the same lessons and exercises to multiple areas of your life.

*If you are currently using online dating or dating apps, look for the book titled "**The Dating App Confessions**" as it might give you better insight into the world of dating apps.*

Contents

Preface

If your dating life has been a mess, don't worry. There's nothing wrong with you. There's nothing wrong with the opposite or same sex. There's nothing wrong with the dating experience. The bottom line is: the dating experience has changed, and that is something we must all accept. This mindfulness program will help you approach dating from a much better perspective, so that you can live your best life possible in the present moment. Whether or not you're currently dating, this mindfulness guide can be a great asset to your personal growth. Don't let dating be a stress, worry, or problem any longer.

The following pages involve a 30 day mindfulness program made up of lessons and exercises to help you overcome patterns of thinking, feeling, and habits that have kept you stuck in an unhealthy dating experience. Though these lessons and exercises can be applied to any attachment, this program will focus specifically on dating.

For some readers, they'll overcome their old perspective quickly and will move on; and for others, they'll reach a better dating experience slowly and gradually. In either case, if you stick with the program, you'll start to witness your experience change for the better. Please don't judge your progress in the program, as this isn't a competition and there isn't a goal you must attain. Let the unhealthy thoughts, feelings, habits, and dependency simply drop as you work through the exercises and lessons.

It's not necessary to complete the program's days in order, nor should you be religious about completing them successfully. There is no such thing as a successful completion of this program. The bottom line is to observe and awaken, and that cannot be obtained through success, force, pressure, struggle, or competition. Simply relax, follow the program, and the grip of your old dating experience will loosen.

You'll also notice that mindfulness, silence, and stillness are a regular discipline for each day in the program. Because you've been influenced by a dependency based society that demands instant gratification, silence and stillness may seem nearly impossible for you to practice. For this reason, we'll incorporate this discipline from the outset. A quiet and still mind is an incredibly powerful resource, but one that requires daily maintenance.

It should also be noted that you're not required to stop dating during the program; however, if you've stopped dating, then it's recommended that you stay single until you've completed the exercises and lessons. The point being: by practicing the following exercises and lessons in the days to come, you won't even need willpower to drop the old dating perspective – it'll just happen.

You'll need about 15-30 minutes per day for the program; but feel free to spend more time if needed. The amount of time doesn't matter, as long as you're in an environment that allows you to concentrate without distraction. Also to be mentioned, the last portion of this book includes note pages that you can use with the exercises. It's encouraged that you write down any thoughts, insights, adaptations, lessons, mantras, etc, on those blank pages. The note pages can also be used to rip out and take with you. Feel free to use them as you wish.

One last thing: If you're like most people, you might be dependent on caffeine, alcohol, or sugar to some extent. If you are, do your best to lessen the consumption of these substances over the next 30 days. It's not necessary that you abstain, but can you cut consumption of these substances in half, or more? It's important that your mind is sober and your body relaxed to make the most of these exercises and lessons.

Let's get started.

Let others know you're practicing mindfulness! Post a picture of the cover and include #30DaysNow. Also, don't forget that each exercise has a unique hashtag for online sharing.

Share your journey and discover other people practicing mindfulness!

Day 1
Exercise:

Find a place without distraction, and turn off all electronics. Sit with your back straight, kneel, or lie on a hard surface (not bed) and remain in silence for 10 minutes.

During these 10 minutes, take deep and focused breaths and hold them for a few seconds each. Exhale slowly. Listen intently to your breathing. Don't try to change it – simply listen, and feel the air go in and out.

*When you're ready, repeat the mantra: "**Be still. Be silent.**" Repeat this slowly multiple times out loud as well as quietly. You might experience boredom or anxiety, but continue repeating the mantra regardless. Repeat it until you're calm and focused. You can continue the deep breathing during the mantra, or take deep breaths during pauses. Don't rush.*

Each of the 30 days will have this time of silence, focused breathing, and a mantra. Except for this page, the end of each day will remind you of the minutes you are to spend in silence and focused breathing; and will also have a mantra for you to practice. You can repeat the mantras during your times of silence and focused breathing, or following. Remember, there is no right or wrong way to do this.

Adverse thoughts and feelings want to fight; in fact, they're energized by fighting. Instead of fighting your internal responses to an unhealthy dating experience, meet them with silence and observation. Let the exercises and lessons in this program guide you.

Day 2

Exercise:

Ponder this question: What is it about dating that has brought you unhappiness, discomfort, or anxiety?

Writing is extremely beneficial to the mind; especially when pondering. Write down your thoughts about this question. If your mind drifts, then write whatever thoughts emerge. It's okay if you have nothing to write, but ponder the question regardless.

If you're like most daters, you find the experience stressful, tiring, hopeless, unpleasant, and possibly boring. Pursuing an intimate human connection has become a difficult task; sort of like a job that brings little happiness or reward. Why do anything that doesn't enhance your present moment happiness?

Very few people find dating enjoyable, which is a clear indication that it's not worth doing, or it's being done through an unhealthy perspective. Hopefully by the end of this program, you'll have a different perspective on dating – so that you can live a happy life while pursuing an intimate connection.

Whatever is your current dating perspective, it's time to drop it and discover your present moment happiness in its absence. Even if you have been dating the same way for years, it's time to drop and unlearn your dating habits and attachments. It's time to awaken and move on.

*10 minutes of silence and focused breathing. Repeat the mantra: ***"Drop. Unlearn. Discover."***

Day 3

Exercise:

On a sheet of paper (any size) write down all the internal lies that you regularly hear about yourself – i.e. within your mind.

Now, tear the paper into multiple pieces, and throw away.

It's common to have an internal voice (or voices) within your mind, playing a record of lies over and over. We eventually begin to accept these lies and let them impact our growth and happiness. Most people you see on a daily basis have these recurring internal voices; and most people are oblivious to them – sort of like white noise. This isn't a mental illness, but a way in which the mind works. We all experience these internal quiet voices whispering untruths about our being. These lies are nothing to fear, but they need to be observed. Writing them down can help you observe and become aware of their deceptions.

The power of silence, focused breathing, and mantras, which you have been practicing, is to draw out the lies. Let them manifest, and observe them. Common internal lies include: *"You can't hold a relationship," "You'll never find another person to love," "You are worthless. No one likes you," "You'll always be alone," "You're a burden,"* and so on. These thoughts are not part of you; however, the deception is to make you believe they are. An unhealthy dating experience and perspective can implant many of these lies clandestinely.

*10 minutes of silence and focused breathing. Repeat the mantra: **"Thoughts are only thoughts - nothing more."**

Day 4

Exercise:

On a piece of paper, write down all the labels and adjectives that you and others use to identify you.

For example, do you see yourself as a daughter, son, mother, father, student, teacher, cashier, friend, engineer, accountant, employee, employer, roommate, wife, husband, etc? And what adjectives do you use to label yourself; for example, do you identify yourself as failed, successful, happy, depressed, good, moral, unethical, lustful, greedy, valuable, worthless, etc? Don't only write down the labels and descriptions you perceive; but also write down what you believe others label you as: do you believe others see you as a loyal girlfriend, great boyfriend, valuable friend, stupid and incompetent employee, extremely smart and talented worker, etc? Take as long as you need, and fill up a sheet of paper with those labels and descriptions.

After you've done that, tear the paper into multiple pieces and throw it away. Those labels and adjectives mean nothing. They're not *you*. You cannot be defined, labeled, described, or controlled by titles. Most people poison their conscience with such learned vocabulary. They really believe these words hold power – they'll even fight, stress out, become ill, and die to make these words part of reality. Dating expectations and adverse attachments, as well as most unhealthy perspectives, teach you to identify with particular words, which are only thoughts. Unlearn them.

*10 minutes of silence and focused breathing. Repeat the mantra: *"**I am not a label, title, or description.**"*

Day 5
(Share this experience using #30DaysBody)

Exercise:

Observe your body. Observe how it feels, moves, and reacts. More direction is explained below.

If you're still dating as you normally have been, or feeling the aftereffects of a poor dating experience, observe your body movements, sounds, sensations, and breaths while you're in the experience. Do your eyes look tired or alert? Do you move your body fast or slow? What's the tone of your voice? Are your breaths short and hurried, or deep and focused? How is your posture? How do you sleep and eat? Try to observe everything about your body while dating from an unhealthy perspective. If you're going on dates, pay close attention to your body's sensations while you're with the other person. Be aware of the experience's affect on your body.

If you're not dating at this time, or you're not feeling the adverse effects of a bad dating experience, then continue with the 10 minutes of silence and focused breathing, but get in touch with your body. A good way to do this is by touching each body part and saying its name, leaving your hand on the part for a few seconds and feeling its texture and warmth. Start with your head: place your hand on your head and say, "*I am touching my head.*" And then work your way down to your shoulders, arms, stomach, legs, knees, and feet. Focus your attention on one body part at a time. Say its name and describe what you are touching.

*10 minutes of silence and focused breathing. Repeat the mantra: "*I am not my body.*"

Day 6

Exercise:

Compliment a total stranger today. You can compliment a cashier, service provider over the phone, server, barista, person at the gym or grocery store, someone on the bus or train, or whomever. It's best if you are not attracted to the person in any way. Compliment someone that you normally wouldn't compliment.

For many people, kindness doesn't come easy. We are taught to judge and avoid from a very early age. You may be a kind person with a good heart; but you're fooling yourself if you believe you treat everyone the same. Spend a few moments today complimenting people you normally wouldn't - not because you dislike them, but because they escape your radar for whatever reason.

Oftentimes, dating impacts our judgments. We expect a lot from the people we date, and those expectations can impede our natural desire to help, serve, and be gracious to others. Forget about dating, and pay attention to all of the people around you. There are many opportunities to put judgments and expectations on the side, so that you can make someone's day better.

It feels good to compliment people, especially when they're overlooked, excluded, and not normally on your radar. Kindness is a self healer, and can help establish a better perspective of relationships. If you're interested in having positive relationships, practice kindness daily.

*10 minutes of silence and focused breathing. Repeat the mantra: **"Kindness heals."***

Day 7

Exercise:

On a piece of paper (any size) write down the goals that you've been striving to achieve – i.e. the dating goals that you believe will bring you fulfillment. For example: finding new love, getting married, traveling the world with a partner, starting a family, finding new friends, building a network, obtaining security, settling down, etc.

Now, tear up the paper into multiple pieces and throw it away.

Goals can be very helpful and useful if they're not obsessed over. However, in the modern world people develop a reliance on goals. Think about all the times you've said something like, "*I need to get that*," "*I must reach this*," "*I'll do anything to accomplish that*", etc. It's often the case that people spend more time worrying about their goals, than freely doing something in the present moment to reach them. Plus, the goal in itself is fleeting, while the journey in the present moment is real and lasting.

The habit of thinking that goals must be met, or else failure ensues, is subtly fixed to dependencies. Since you've been dating, what have been your short-term and long-term goals? What was it that you felt you needed to achieve via those dates? Let those goals go; new ones will appear in the present moment.

*10 minutes of silence and focused breathing. Repeat the mantra: "**My happiness does not depend on meeting a goal. I'm happy now.**"

Day 8

Exercise:

Stand in front of a doorway, with the door open. Close your eyes, and take a deep breath. With eyes closed and holding your breath, step through the doorway. Once you have stepped through completely, open your eyes and exhale.

Doorways offer great lessons for practicing mindfulness and observation. How often do you rush through doors without paying attention to the change of environment? We don't often pay attention or appreciate the transition; we simply rush through unaware that our perspective has changed. This isn't a bad thing; in fact, it's great that we don't stall in front of doorways, too afraid to enter the next environment. At the beginning of this exercise you were in a particular place, and then you stepped through a doorway into a completely different setting. You made a transition without worry or concern, and very naturally.

When it comes to physical doorways, we rarely stop and worry about the change of environment – we just walk through and accept the new experience. You can apply this same lesson to decisions that have you stressed, anxious, or worried regarding the dating experience. Step through the decision to stop unhealthy dating, and accept the change; but try to step through aware and grateful. There will always be a doorway leading to new experiences and perspectives. When you drop your old dating perspective, new doorways will be present.

*10 minutes of silence and focused breathing. Repeat the mantra: **"I accept change with awareness and gratitude."**

Day 9

Exercise:

Find a hard object that you can hold in the palm of your hand (such as a stone, ball, or bottle). With either hand, grip this object tightly and squeeze it as hard as you can. Squeeze it forcefully until you can't hold onto it any longer. Drop the object when ready.

If you could continue squeezing that object forever, perhaps you would; but your muscles and nerves can only endure for so long. At some point, you simply and quickly release the grip and drop the object. There isn't a process to the drop; it just happens when your body says that's enough. The release happens naturally without effort.

Too often, we hold tightly to views and expectations of dating that are unhealthy and impede present moment happiness. People become addicted to certain approaches to dating, hopelessly looking for *the one* - or at least someone who's as close to *the one* as possible. If you're still holding onto a specific view of dating and *the one*, then it's time to loosen your grip and let it drop.

Letting go of an unhealthy dependency, habit, thought pattern, addiction, emotion, or behavior can be that easy. Letting go can be as natural and guilt free as dropping the object you were gripping onto so tightly in this exercise; so, take a lesson from your body's experience. When it's time to let go, then let go. The time to let go is always now

*10 minutes of silence and focused breathing. Repeat the mantra: **"Letting go is natural. I can let go, here and now."**

Day 10

Exercise:

Focus on a natural object or scene for 10 minutes, without distraction and in silence.

Focusing on a natural object for an extended period of time is an ancient practice. How often have you stopped to observe something objectively for more than 10 minutes? When was the last time you've quietly watched a sunset, sunrise, tree sway in the wind, bird chirping, clouds passing or expanding, or just a rock? That might sound boring, but this practice is very liberating. If you look at anything long enough, you start to see it from a different perspective. As easy as this exercise sounds, it's not – try it out, and see how long you can observe without thoughts impeding the practice.

Watching a bird feed may be more interesting than watching an immobile rock; but I encourage you to start with an immobile object, such as a stone or piece of wood. During this process thoughts will emerge – observe the thoughts and let them pass. Don't attach a goal or benchmark of success to this exercise; just observe an object.

The goal of an unhealthy dating perspective is to hypnotize you with a false narrative; stealing your attention from the present. Wake up to what's around you in the present.

*10 minutes of silence and focused breathing. Repeat the mantra: **"Be focused. Observe. Be present."**

Day 11

Exercise:

Listen to a person intently without interruption. Only speak if the person asks you a question, but don't give a long answer. Make the conversation entirely theirs. Give them the floor, and listen to every word they are saying. Again, do not interrupt. Observe their words and facial expressions without judgment. Be patient and relaxed, even if they speak for more than a few minutes.

Patience is a dying practice in our digital age. It appears that all business involves the perceived need to go faster, faster, and faster. Quicker responses, faster uploads, more data, rapid analysis, accelerated transportation, and all sorts of chop-chop. This false need for speed has seeped deep into our collective psyche. The modern world is filled with anxiously demanding people, going nowhere fast.

This widespread lack of patience has caused a problem with regard to listening to one another. It has also caused dependency on fast dating to manifest extensively. People who are dependent on a quick dating approach require the experience to happen at lightning speed. Practicing patience by listening intently to someone speak is a great way to slow down the mind and build meaningful relationships. The unhealthy perspective of quick dating cannot compete with real human interaction, which requires patience.

*10 minutes of silence and focused breathing. Repeat the mantra: **"Listen. Be patient. Listen."**

Day 12

(Share this experience using #30DaysBreak)

Exercise:

Find an object that you can break: an egg, a drinking glass, a pencil...anything. In a safe place, break the object of your choice, and be especially careful if it's glass or something sharp.

Don't clean up the pieces immediately, observe the mess and let the pieces sit for at least a few minutes.

Did you break the object, or did I break the object by directing you to break it? And if you believe it was only you who broke the object, did the object allow you to break it? This isn't an exercise meant to release frustration or stress. The purpose of this lesson is to show you that you're not 100% responsible for your perceived chaos, mess, loss, or broken pieces.

Destruction happens in the present moment, and that's OK. We spend so much time worrying about goals, relationships, jobs, situations, the future, and other things breaking into pieces. And when that happens, we tend to blame ourselves or others, because that's what we've been taught to do. Allow breaking to happen; and observe the pieces as well as your reaction to the destruction.

Dating is rarely a perfect fairy tale experience. Most of the time it's confusing, messy, and uncertain; and that's OK. When you start dating from a perspective of detachment, happiness, and present moment awareness, you'll be OK with the broken pieces.

*10 minutes of silence and focused breathing. Repeat the mantra: **"I cannot harm or break the present moment."**

Day 13

Exercise:

Hold a smile for 5 minutes. You don't need to do this exercise in front of a mirror; but feel free to do so if you wish. You can even do this exercise during the 10 minutes of silence and focused breathing. While holding your smile, take a moment and feel your face; actually touch the smile and the curvature of your lips and cheek bones.

Have you ever behaved a certain way and then saw your mood change immediately? Physical exercise, such as running and weightlifting, does this for many people. Certain forms of yoga have also been used by people to change their moods. The point is: changing your behavior not only impacts other people, but can also impact your perception of yourself.

You'll notice that while you're smiling during this exercise, you may experience certain emotions. You might feel silly, embarrassed, stupid, funny, weird, or whatever. Continue smiling regardless. In fact, if you're still experiencing adverse feelings from an unhealthy dating perspective, smile while you're in the grips of them – hold the smile as long as you can; set a reminder alarm if needed. As always, observe your thoughts while you're smiling; observe the thoughts as if they're clouds passing by in a bright blue sky.

*10 minutes of silence and focused breathing. Repeat the mantra: *"Happiness is now. I am happy."*

Day 14

Exercise:

Most food products have a "Nutritious Facts" label that will tell you the percentage of fat, cholesterol, sodium, carbohydrates, protein, and other important nutritious content in the product. Let's make one for your experience.

On a sheet of paper, write down the words: happiness, stress, anxiety, worry, anger, and depression. Feel free to add other words that describe emotions and feelings that you may regularly experience. Now, next to each word write down the percentages that best represent their measure in your life. There is no right or wrong for this exercise; the point is to become keenly aware of what emotions and feelings you are experiencing more often than others. If you write 70% depression, that is not "bad". Simply be honest with the percentages; recognize them.

Which emotions received the highest percentages? Which received the lowest? Remember, you are not your emotions or feelings; however, you do experience emotions and feelings, and some of them will be experienced more than others, especially during an unhealthy dating experience. If you are experiencing adverse emotions more often than positive ones, then don't let that bother you. Whatever emotion you experience in the present moment, observe it and let it pass. For the negative emotions that come regularly, examine them and let them fade. Observation is the key to understanding.

*10 minutes of silence and focused breathing. Repeat the mantra: **"I am not ruled by emotion. I am here and now."**

Day 15

Exercise:

Choose a song to listen to carefully. You can choose the song from your music collection; or simply turn on the radio and wait for a song to play.

While listening to the song, don't listen to the notes, beats, voice, or rhythm; instead, listen for the silence between sounds. Listen for the stops, pauses, and absence of sound between notes. Listen for the silence in the song.

Have you ever realized that your favorite songs would not exist without silence? Every note, rhythm, beat, and voice needs a moment of silence to manifest – even if that moment exists in a millisecond. Without silence, there would be no noise, yet alone music. This isn't to say that noise and silence are in conflict; quite the opposite actually. Sounds and silence are complementary. So, were you able to hear the silence within the song? Practice this repeatedly whenever you listen to music. Listen for the silence that allows the music to endure.

Similarly, we need silence to let the rhythm of life manifest. Unfortunately, this has become a struggle for many people, because we live in an unbalanced world that encourages sound over silence. Don't listen to the noise of a poor dating experience, and don't fear silence. Silence is a powerful remedy. Practice remaining in silence daily; you'll start to hear and see new and wonderful things.

*10 minutes of silence and focused breathing. Repeat the mantra: **"Be silent. Listen. Be silent."***

Day 16

Exercise:

On a piece of paper (any size) write down the name of your current emotion. For example, at this moment you might be feeling agitated, calm, bored, angry, anxious, excited, etc. Whatever emotion you are experiencing, give it a name and put it on paper.

Now, write down "I'm experiencing this emotion in the present moment and it will pass. It's only an emotion."

You can throw the paper away, or hold onto it if you wish.

Similar to how we give certain words credence, we tend to give our emotions a lot of trust. We also tend to blame the outside world for emotions we are feeling: *"They made me angry," "I'm depressed because they didn't want me," "If they gave me the job, I would be happy."*

The emotions you feel are in you, not in the outer world. No one can cause you to feel or emote in a particular way; if they're able to, it's only because you let them. A great way to let a harmful emotion pass is to observe it; and a good start is by giving it a name and seeing it as powerless.

It's commonplace to blame others for our pain. Instead of seeing the emotion for what it is and letting it pass, we've been taught to rely on attachments, like dating, to manage the emotional reaction. Wake up! Emotions are not you.

*15 minutes of silence and focused breathing. Repeat the mantra: **"I am not an emotion. All emotions pass."**

Day 17

Exercise:

Choose an object that you use and rely on every day, and that you sometimes lose – such as a key, cell phone, pen, hat, toothbrush, or television controller.

Now, actually attempt to lose this object. Hide it well, and try to make yourself forget where it is.

More than likely you won't be able to lose this object, as hard as you try, because you have applied a lot of attention to the process of losing it and trying to make yourself forget. At this point, losing it is nearly impossible. Why do you think this is?

If you try to drop a dependency, behavior, thought pattern, addiction, or any unhealthy vice using a lot of thought, attention, focus, struggle, and effort…you'll never lose it. It will be with you in one form or another for a very long time, possibly forever. The point is: whatever you give attention to consistently, will be difficult to lose. This is the reason why people who complain a lot are never happy – they can't stop giving thought and attention to the problems they're grumbling about. The problems eventually become an intimate part of their lives. Remember, rival enemies maintain a devoted relationship.

Don't think about past dating experiences, approaches, and perspectives; don't struggle, fight, or oppose them. Let them be forgotten, and thus lost.

*15 minutes of silence and focused breathing. Repeat the mantra: **"I do not need to hold on. I allow it to be lost."**

(23)

Day 18

Exercise:

Say the words "Guilt", "Shame", and "Regret" 10 times to yourself out loud. Don't rush. Pause between each repetition. For the pause, you can take a deep breath. Your eyes can remain open or closed. Again, don't rush - say the words slowly and observe any thoughts, feelings, or images that emerge internally.

Now, say these words again 10 times, but with a smile.

What futile credence we give words such as Guilt, Shame and Regret. We use these words on ourselves as well as others; they become regular vocabulary for our internal recurring voices. And in the end, they're mere words that hold no power. What would these words be without a facial expression, tone, inflection, or emphasis?

When you said these three specific words, what thoughts came to mind, what did you feel, and was there a reaction in your body? If there is a reaction, such as shortness of breath or a frown, people tend to interpret it as sadness; but this reaction is a learned behavior. We've been taught to feel and think a certain way with regard to guilt, shame, and regret. The truth is: these words mean nothing.

An unhealthy dating perspective, like most adverse views, flourishes on these three words and the learned reactions they produce. But see them for what they are…mere words with no power.

*15 minutes of silence and focused breathing. Repeat the mantra: **"I am not Guilt, Shame, or Regret."***

Day 19

Exercise:

Take a piece of paper (any size, but large enough to draw on); with a pen, scribble a random line with your eyes closed. Don't lift your pen from the paper; keep it as one messy scribble. Only spend two or three seconds doing this.

Now, with your eyes open and seeing what your scribble looks like, make it into an actual image of something. Work with the scribble to make something noticeable.

What did you make out of your scribble: an animal, house, drifting balloon, kite, a person, a scenario, an entire scene with many things, etc?

This is one of my favorite exercises. It's a lesson that teaches that the scribbles and confusions we experience in life can be changed and formed with a new perspective. Life is all about perspective. How do you perceive scribble, mess, chaos, clutter, disarray, and confusion in your life experience? Do you know that you can perceive it differently starting now?

In silence, stillness, and with an open mind, take a look at any scribbles that you may be experiencing in life, with and without regard to dating. If you observe long enough, without judgment, you'll gain a new perspective.

*15 minutes of silence and focused breathing. Repeat the mantra: **"I am not confused. My perception can always change in the present moment."**

Day 20

Exercise:

Choose a physical symbol that will remind you to observe and be aware in the present moment. Try to choose something from nature, or that is made of natural material.

The object you choose can be anything, but it's best if it's something that you can enjoy looking at and touching. For example, many walkers and hikers will find a unique rock small enough to carry in their hands. A stone, necklace, bracelet, seashell, cedar block, coin…anything will do, as long as you enjoy it and you can dedicate it as a tool for remembrance.

Another cunning trick of an adverse dating perspective is to confuse the mind into forgetting you're part of the natural world. Relationship memories prey on, manipulate, and influence the imagination. Thus, you're taken out of physical reality. By having a symbol of remembrance, you can reconnect with the present moment. This symbol isn't meant to be an idol, god, or icon. Don't think too deeply into this. The symbol is simply a tool to help you remember where you are in the here and now. As long as you're aware of the present, you'll have no desire to return to an unhealthy attachment to dating.

*15 minutes of silence and focused breathing. Repeat the mantra: *__*"All is well. Here and now, all is well."*__

Day 21

Exercise:

Find a coin. While standing, flip the coin and let it land wherever. If it lands with the head side up, spin around to the right until you come back to your original place; if it lands tail side up, spin around to the left until you come back to your original place. Again, head side up, spin to the right; tail side up, spin to the left – doing a full circle until you return to your original standing position.

In which direction did you spin? In this exercise you left the direction of your movement completely up to the flip, the coin, and gravity. When you spun, you experienced a specific visual perception of the environment that you would not have had from spinning in the opposite direction. But, you returned to the original position regardless, full circle.

The experience would have been different if you spun to the opposite side; and if you repeat this exercise multiple times, your experiences in the same direction will be different as well. The point being: it doesn't matter what direction you go in or what you experience; you'll always return to the present moment; so the time to be awake, aware, and happy is always now.

Whatever happens with regard to your dating experiences, you will always have access to the present moment, so enjoy being here and now. Dating concerns don't command the present. When you date, date in the present moment.

*15 minutes of silence and focused breathing. Repeat the mantra: **"The direction does not matter. I am always here and now, in the present moment."***

(27)

Day 22

Exercise:

On a sheet of paper (one that you can easily save and return to later) make a list of hobbies that you've had in the past but have neglected, and also make a list of hobbies that you would like to start in the future.

From these lists choose one hobby from the past and one new hobby that you'd like to start. Focus only on these two – the old hobby and the new one. Make this a priority.

How often have you said, or have heard other people say, "*I wish I had the time.*" You do have the time. You just choose to think of time in the way that you've been taught to perceive it. If your life depended on it, you would certainly make the time if needed.

In fact, time is a manmade construct - don't ever forget that. There is only the present moment. Past and future are not here and now. We spend far too much time thinking about time. How many of your recurrent inner thoughts involve questions such as, "*When will that ever happen?*" "*When will I ever change?*" "*Why did that have to happen?*" "*If the past were different, life would be better.*" These are lies that only eat into the present moment, and infect our modern world.

Quick, excessive, desperate, stressful, impatient, obsessive, and unhealthy dating can occupy and steal your present moment awareness; and that moment could be used to pursue hobbies that magnify your happiness.

*15 minutes of silence and focused breathing. Repeat the mantra: "**The time is now. Happiness is present.**"

(28)

Day 23

Exercise:

Pinch the skin on the back of your hand or forearm until there is discomfort and slight pain. It's not necessary to pinch hard enough to bruise yourself, just enough to feel a small burn.

Did I cause the pain by asking you to do this exercise? No; you caused this pain to yourself – think about this carefully. You even decided how much pain to give yourself, and when to relieve the pain. You can't blame me or anyone else for the pain you just experienced. You were solely responsible. You were also responsible for letting go.

This is easily understood with regard to physical pain, such as pinching oneself; however, we have a lot of difficulty understanding this lesson as it applies to adverse emotions and feelings. How often have you said, and have heard others say, *"He makes me so angry when...",* "I'm *depressed because she...",* or *"I'm so frustrated that they..."* No person ever makes you experience negative feelings, even while dating. It's always you who are experiencing them; and then placing the blame on others. Essentially, you are emotionally pinching yourself and not letting go.

People go their entire lives without releasing the pinch. Instead of letting go, they scream at others, *"Release the pain! Let go! Fix this! Stop this! You're to blame!"* Wake up and see that you are solely responsible for letting go of the pain, and you can do it now.

*15 minutes of silence and focused breathing. Repeat the mantra: **"I can release negative feelings, here and now."**

Day 24

Exercise:

Choose a book; perhaps one that you have at home that you haven't read in a while, or from the library. You can also use a long article for this exercise. It's best if you haven't read the book or article beforehand.

Now, instead of reading from the beginning; read the last chapter (or paragraph if it's an article) first.

Does this go against your conventional way of perceiving a story? Did you feel that it's pointless to even read the entire book, or article, since you're aware of its ending before reading the beginning? Just because you started at the end of the book doesn't impact the story; instead, it impacts your perception.

If you've been struggling with bad dating experiences for a while; is it the beginning, middle, or end of your dilemma? This isn't to teach you that you can control the end or beginning of an experience; because you can't. The purpose is to show you that the present moment is all you'll ever need, and you can accept the end as the beginning and the beginning as the end, if that's your experience in the present moment. So, be open to perceive all things as they are now, with or without a beginning or end. In other words, be awake, don't worry, and be happy.

*15 minutes of silence and focused breathing. Repeat the mantra: **"There is no end or beginning. There's only ever now."**

Day 25

Exercise:

Write a letter or email to yourself. There is something about using pen and paper that is very effective when writing letters, but feel free to write an email if you wish. Don't send the letter or email, just write it and save it for a day – you can toss it out or delete it tomorrow.

Write anything that comes to mind: It can be advice you want to give yourself, a story from the past, random thoughts and feelings about dating, frustrations and worries, things you're thankful for, etc. There is no right or wrong – write whatever comes to mind in the moment. Try to write at least two full paragraphs..

What was the theme and voice of your message? Was it a positive or negative tone? Were you advising yourself? Did you make any judgments about yourself? Did you start demanding that you should or should not do something? Was the letter full of gratitude? Was there anger and despair? Read the letter as if you were reading it from a friend – is it a letter that would upset you, or one that you would welcome with excitement and a smile?

Whatever you wrote is essentially being written on the tablet of your mind. This exercise is useful for getting to know the internal voice that we all have in our minds. It's an internal voice that can change for the better with observation, acceptance, and awareness. Be aware of your internal voice in the present moment.

*15 minutes of silence and focused breathing. Repeat the mantra: *"**I am not my internal voice. I am aware.**"*

Day 26

Exercise:

Think of a major worry that consistently upsets you. On a sheet of paper, write down three worst case scenarios for that dominating concern. For example, if someone is persistently worried about dying alone, that individual can write as a worst case scenario, "I will die alone, without anyone at my side, and without family or loved ones to say goodbye." As mentioned, write down three worst case scenarios for the worry. The worry doesn't have to be as extreme as dying alone; use whichever worry hinders you.

Now, next to each of those three worst case scenarios write, "I accept this." You can either toss the paper or keep it.

Worry is an illness that goes untreated in most people, especially while dating. Think of worry like a cancer of the spirit; but few people know how to treat it effectively. One of the only ways to eradicate worry isn't to fight, ignore, or run from it; but to face it in the present moment and accept it for the illusion it is. You can never be worried about something happening in the present moment – that's impossible; you can only be worried about the future, which is always illusory.

Writing down your worries and worst case scenarios, if they ever do come true (which they rarely do), is a great way to draw those thoughts out of your mind and into the present moment, allowing you to face, accept, and observe them.

*15 minutes of silence and focused breathing. Repeat the mantra: ***"Worries are not real. They are only thoughts."***

Day 27

Exercise:

Using objects that can stack (rocks, books, boxes, containers, pillows, etc), stack them slowly and carefully until they fall.

When the stack collapses, smile and laugh.

The lives of many people are spent stacking things for the goal of success, as defined by society. People stack possessions, knowledge, relationships, degrees, money, jobs, toys, businesses, experiences, etc. They stress, fight, fatigue, compete, become ill, and get anxious and depressed through the process of stacking; yet, few people have found happiness. Society tells us that if our stack is high and mighty, we'll have obtained success. What a deception. What are you stacking; or what do you feel compelled to stack? How was your old dating perspective and experiences supporting that stack?

Allow the stack to fall. This lesson is not encouraging complacency; but instead teaches that real, authentic, and fulfilling relationships can only happen apart from the stress and worry of stacking. When you stack, you're focused on the future and the perceived importance of the stack; and then you have to maintain that heap of nonsense, which requires a lot of anxiety and pressure. Focus on your experience in the present moment; and if the stack falls, then smile and laugh.

*15 minutes of silence and focused breathing. Repeat the mantra: **"I allow the stack to fall."**

Day 28

Exercise:

Light a candle and observe its flame for 5 minutes. Watch it move and feel its heat. Appreciate its energy.

Now, blow out the flame.

(If you don't have a candle, light a match and blow it out; and if you don't have a candle or match, stare at a dim light for 5 minutes and then turn it off.)

The temperature of a small candle flame (and match flame) is around 1200 Celsius (which is about 2000 Fahrenheit). That's a lot of energy! And within a fraction of a second, it was extinguished as you blew it out; or in the case of the light, turned off its energy source. There wasn't a gradual process with delays and stops. You blew out the highly energized flame, and that was it - from 1200 Celsius to nonexistent in no time; or should I say, in present no time.

We think that our attachments have so much energy and power. It's not just an attachment to an old and unhealthy dating perspective, but all dependencies survive on this deception of power. The truth is: attachments don't have energy like the candle flame, though your mind may have been tricked into believing they do. The candle flame is real and powerful; whereas dependencies are illusory and fictitious.

As easily and quickly as you extinguished the flame, you can drop an adverse dating perspective.

*15 minutes of silence and focused breathing. Repeat the mantra: **"Dependency isn't real. It can be extinguished."**

Day 29
(Share this experience using #30DaysLaugh)

Exercise:

Make yourself laugh for 5 minutes. Don't stop laughing. You might feel strange, weird, embarrassed, or stupid...it doesn't matter, just laugh. Try to laugh alone and without the aid of a comedy or joke. If you don't know how to start, just start making the noises that typically accompany your laughter.

What feelings did you experience during this exercise? Many people report feeling embarrassed or goofy, which is great; however, most people also report a feeling of relief and buoyancy when they've completed this exercise.

Similar to holding a smile, laughing for 5 minutes is a fantastic way to come into present awareness. If you think about it, humor is necessary for life. How sad is the person who is unable to laugh at the experiences of life? After all, life is funny, even the dreadful and lousy experiences.

If you ever again experience adverse thoughts and feelings that accompany dating, simply laugh at them. Consider how crazy and frivolous your old thoughts and worries about dating, and your reactions to them, are; it really is a funny misperception. The entire situation is comical. If you perceive the old dating attachment for what it truly is - a fictitious, impractical, and frivolous dependency – then it can be easily dropped. You must learn to laugh at it. Genuinely laugh bad dating experiences and perspectives away.

*15 minutes of silence and focused breathing. Repeat the mantra: **"Life is wonderful, funny, and real."**

Day 30
(Share this experience using #30DaysThanks)

Exercise:

Take a piece of paper (one that you can keep) and write down all that you are grateful for – these things don't have to be in any particular order of importance.

Next to each thing you list, write "Thank you."

The person who isn't thankful for all that life gives is typically quite miserable; and dating miseries thrive on that negativity. The truly grateful person can let go of anything at anytime. A thankful person is always a happy person, so practice gratitude daily.

Have you ever heard anyone say, *"I'm so grateful for dating"*? Nobody is thankful for dating; which is a clear sign that it's often an unhealthy attachment. However, a few people have learned to be thankful for the present moment experience and have enjoyed dating without concern or attachment.

Not only is it unhealthy, but dependency on an adverse dating perspective discourages a grateful mind and soul. With only one life to live in the present moment, it's important to always emphasize a grateful heart. Spend time with people who are grateful, and do things that nourish a thankful heart in the present moment. Anything that encourages misery and anxiety isn't worth giving attention to. Be thankful, always.

*15 minutes of silence and focused breathing. Repeat the mantra: *"I am grateful. I am thankful."*

Conclusion

The exercises and lessons in this program taught and encouraged observation, awareness to your present moment experience, change of perception, and awakening to true happiness, which can only be found here and now. You were shown that your negative thoughts and feelings are not caused by dating, or any unhealthy reliance, but are solely within you and illusory; which means that you are capable of letting those thoughts and feelings pass and dropping the old dating perspective in the present moment.

As mentioned at the beginning, there were no goals or measures of success for this program. If you were hoping to find a reason to stop or continue dating, then you may be spending too much time struggling and thinking about dating. This was not meant to be a struggle, but a release.

Life is not meant to be spent with an adverse dating perspective, or any type of unhealthy attachment. Wake up to the present moment and enjoy your present experience. If you've made it through the program, you are certainly more awakened then when you started; however, don't give up mindfully practicing observation of thoughts and feelings, stillness, silence, deep and focused breathing, allowing everything to pass, laughing, smiling, and being grateful.

Live wonderfully awakened and aware…with or without a better dating experience.

Notes for Day 1

(Use this page to write down thoughts, reminders, ideas, prayers, mantras, revelations, lessons, modifications to the exercise, or experiences. If you'd like to share something, please post using **#30DaysNow** or use the exercise's unique hashtag.)

_____

_____

_____

_____

_____

_____

_____

_____

_____

_____

_____

_____

_____

_____

_____

_____

_____

_____

_____

_____

_____

_____

_____

_____

_____

_____

_____

_____

_____

Notes for Day 2

(Use this page to write down thoughts, reminders, ideas, prayers, mantras, revelations, lessons, modifications to the exercise, or experiences. If you'd like to share something, please post using **#30DaysNow** or use the exercise's unique hashtag.)

Notes for Day 3

(Use this page to write down thoughts, reminders, ideas, prayers, mantras, revelations, lessons, modifications to the exercise, or experiences. If you'd like to share something, please post using **#30DaysNow** or use the exercise's unique hashtag.)

_____

_____

_____

_____

_____

_____

_____

_____

_____

_____

_____

_____

_____

_____

_____

_____

_____

_____

_____

_____

_____

_____

_____

_____

_____

_____

_____

_____

Notes for Day 4

(Use this page to write down thoughts, reminders, ideas, prayers, mantras, revelations, lessons, modifications to the exercise, or experiences. If you'd like to share something, please post using **#30DaysNow** or use the exercise's unique hashtag.)

Notes for Day 5

(Use this page to write down thoughts, reminders, ideas, prayers, mantras, revelations, lessons, modifications to the exercise, or experiences. If you'd like to share something, please post using **#30DaysNow** or use the exercise's unique hashtag.)

_____

_____

_____

_____

_____

_____

_____

_____

_____

_____

_____

_____

_____

_____

_____

_____

_____

_____

_____

_____

_____

_____

_____

_____

_____

_____

Notes for Day 6

Notes for Day 7

(Use this page to write down thoughts, reminders, ideas, prayers, mantras, revelations, lessons, modifications to the exercise, or experiences. If you'd like to share something, please post using **#30DaysNow** or use the exercise's unique hashtag.)

Notes for Day 8

(Use this page to write down thoughts, reminders, ideas, prayers, mantras, revelations, lessons, modifications to the exercise, or experiences. If you'd like to share something, please post using **#30DaysNow** or use the exercise's unique hashtag.)

Notes for Day 9

(Use this page to write down thoughts, reminders, ideas, prayers, mantras, revelations, lessons, modifications to the exercise, or experiences. If you'd like to share something, please post using **#30DaysNow** or use the exercise's unique hashtag.)

Notes for Day 10

(Use this page to write down thoughts, reminders, ideas, prayers, mantras, revelations, lessons, modifications to the exercise, or experiences. If you'd like to share something, please post using **#30DaysNow** or use the exercise's unique hashtag.)

Notes for Day 11

(Use this page to write down thoughts, reminders, ideas, prayers, mantras, revelations, lessons, modifications to the exercise, or experiences. If you'd like to share something, please post using **#30DaysNow** or use the exercise's unique hashtag.)

Notes for Day 12

(Use this page to write down thoughts, reminders, ideas, prayers, mantras, revelations, lessons, modifications to the exercise, or experiences. If you'd like to share something, please post using **#30DaysNow** or use the exercise's unique hashtag.)

_____

_____

_____

_____

_____

_____

_____

_____

_____

_____

_____

_____

_____

_____

_____

_____

_____

_____

_____

_____

_____

_____

_____

_____

_____

_____

_____

Notes for Day 13

(Use this page to write down thoughts, reminders, ideas, prayers, mantras, revelations, lessons, modifications to the exercise, or experiences. If you'd like to share something, please post using **#30DaysNow** or use the exercise's unique hashtag.)

_____

_____

_____

_____

_____

_____

_____

_____

_____

_____

_____

_____

_____

_____

_____

_____

_____

_____

_____

_____

_____

_____

_____

_____

_____

_____

_____

_____

_____

_____

Notes for Day 14

(Use this page to write down thoughts, reminders, ideas, prayers, mantras, revelations, lessons, modifications to the exercise, or experiences. If you'd like to share something, please post using **#30DaysNow** or use the exercise's unique hashtag.)

Notes for Day 15

(Use this page to write down thoughts, reminders, ideas, prayers, mantras, revelations, lessons, modifications to the exercise, or experiences. If you'd like to share something, please post using **#30DaysNow** or use the exercise's unique hashtag.)

Notes for Day 16

(Use this page to write down thoughts, reminders, ideas, prayers, mantras, revelations, lessons, modifications to the exercise, or experiences. If you'd like to share something, please post using **#30DaysNow** or use the exercise's unique hashtag.)

Notes for Day 17

(Use this page to write down thoughts, reminders, ideas, prayers, mantras, revelations, lessons, modifications to the exercise, or experiences. If you'd like to share something, please post using **#30DaysNow** or use the exercise's unique hashtag.)

_____

_____

_____

_____

_____

_____

_____

_____

_____

_____

_____

_____

_____

_____

_____

_____

_____

_____

_____

_____

_____

_____

_____

_____

_____

_____

_____

_____

Notes for Day 18

(Use this page to write down thoughts, reminders, ideas, prayers, mantras, revelations, lessons, modifications to the exercise, or experiences. If you'd like to share something, please post using #30DaysNow or use the exercise's unique hashtag.)

Notes for Day 19

(Use this page to write down thoughts, reminders, ideas, prayers, mantras, revelations, lessons, modifications to the exercise, or experiences. If you'd like to share something, please post using **#30DaysNow** or use the exercise's unique hashtag.)

Notes for Day 20

(Use this page to write down thoughts, reminders, ideas, prayers, mantras, revelations, lessons, modifications to the exercise, or experiences. If you'd like to share something, please post using **#30DaysNow** or use the exercise's unique hashtag.)

Notes for Day 21

(Use this page to write down thoughts, reminders, ideas, prayers, mantras, revelations, lessons, modifications to the exercise, or experiences. If you'd like to share something, please post using **#30DaysNow** or use the exercise's unique hashtag.)

Notes for Day 22

(Use this page to write down thoughts, reminders, ideas, prayers, mantras, revelations, lessons, modifications to the exercise, or experiences. If you'd like to share something, please post using **#30DaysNow** or use the exercise's unique hashtag.)

Notes for Day 23

Notes for Day 24

(Use this page to write down thoughts, reminders, ideas, prayers, mantras, revelations, lessons, modifications to the exercise, or experiences. If you'd like to share something, please post using **#30DaysNow** or use the exercise's unique hashtag.)

Notes for Day 25

(Use this page to write down thoughts, reminders, ideas, prayers, mantras, revelations, lessons, modifications to the exercise, or experiences. If you'd like to share something, please post using #30DaysNow or use the exercise's unique hashtag.)

Notes for Day 26

(Use this page to write down thoughts, reminders, ideas, prayers, mantras, revelations, lessons, modifications to the exercise, or experiences. If you'd like to share online, please post using **#30DaysNow** or use the exercise's unique hashtag.)

Notes for Day 27

(Use this page to write down thoughts, reminders, ideas, prayers, mantras, revelations, lessons, modifications to the exercise, or experiences. If you'd like to share something, please post using **#30DaysNow** or use the exercise's unique hashtag.)

Notes for Day 28

(Use this page to write down thoughts, reminders, ideas, prayers, mantras, revelations, lessons, modifications to the exercise, or experiences. If you'd like to share something, please post using #30DaysNow or use the exercise's unique hashtag.)

Notes for Day 29

(Use this page to write down thoughts, reminders, ideas, prayers, mantras, revelations, lessons, modifications to the exercise, or experiences. If you'd like to share something, please post using **#30DaysNow** or use the exercise's unique hashtag.)

Notes for Day 30

(Use this page to write down thoughts, reminders, ideas, prayers, mantras, revelations, lessons, modifications to the exercise, or experiences. If you'd like to share something, please post using **#30DaysNow** or use the exercise's unique hashtag.)

To be mindful is to experience life in the present moment...it's the only moment we have.

*If you are currently using online dating or dating apps, look for the book titled "**The Dating App Confessions**" as it might give you better insight into the world of dating apps.*

Don't forget to leave an online review.

Thank you!

Made in the USA
Las Vegas, NV
02 June 2022